Food for Our Great Journey

Life is often compared to a great journey. We might imagine we are traveling a road that twists and turns, climbs mountains, and meanders through peaceful valleys. Life's "highway" takes us through a little of everything. In order to develop this analogy, recall a particularly beautiful highway or road that you have traveled. It does not matter if you journeyed by car, bike, or foot. Using as much detail as possible, describe this road and its surroundings. What made it unusual or striking? Where was the road and where was it leading you? What time of year was it? Was the road difficult or pleasurable—or both?

_____
_____
_____
_____
_____
_____
_____
_____
_____
_____
_____
_____
_____

For many, adolescence is one of the more "mountainous" parts of life's great journey. It is a time when young people take a giant (and often painful) step toward maturity. It is a period of transition from dependent childhood to a more responsible and independent adulthood.

In his Gospel, Saint Luke makes reference to the mountains and valleys in our lives. Using the words of the prophet Isaiah, Luke tells of a "baptism of repentance" and a faith in the Lord Jesus which will change the course of our lives forever:

"Every valley shall be filled, and every mountain and hill shall be made low, and the crooked shall be made straight, and the rough ways made smooth; and all flesh shall see the salvation of God."
Luke 3:5-6

Think for a moment about your life right now. Is the pathway "smooth"? Or is it full of mountains and valleys? Try to be specific and write about particularly troubling "mountains," or times when you feel unusually low. (In the weeks ahead, you will learn more about how the sacrament of confirmation serves as "food" for our great journey.)

_____
_____
_____
_____
_____
_____
_____
_____
_____
_____
_____

What does it mean to be a "child of God"? What meaning does your baptism have for you today? The oil (chrism) of our baptism reminds us that we are priest, prophet, and king, yet our society defines our values in many **destructive** ways. Give two examples of how our modern world defines our values.

The Parish Commitment Ceremony

Community is very important in Christian life. It is through others that we come to know God. While the creative power and majesty of God are made apparent to us through the magnificence of nature, it is only through human community that we come to know God's compassion, kindness, mercy, generosity, and love. Jesus commanded us to love one another because he knew that when we share unconditional love, we come to see the face of God.

Let's begin by bringing to mind our membership in the most basic human community—the family. Think about your family for a few moments.

Briefly describe the members of your immediate family:

_____

_____

_____

_____

Describe any significant members of your extended family, especially those living with you:

_____

_____

_____

_____

In what ways do you contribute to the healthy functioning of your family? (Think not only in terms of duties and chores, but describe ways you support various members emotionally and spiritually.)

_____

_____

_____

_____

You have lived with your family for many years, and you know its strengths and weaknesses. Briefly describe one or two really positive aspects of your family. Then write about an area you would like to see improve. (Again, focus primarily on the relationships within your family unit.)

_____
_____
_____
_____
_____
_____
_____
_____
_____
_____
_____
_____
_____
_____
_____
_____
_____
_____

Now think about another form of community—your "circle of friends." Are you a person who prefers the company of just one or two trusted friends? Or are you a person who loves to be part of a group? Whether it be large, small, or somewhere in between, friendship "communities" tend to become very important during adolescence. Friends are often a great support—and often the source of much tension and pain.

Generally speaking, real friends fill our lives with positive experiences, and they work hard to make us feel good about ourselves. Real friends tend to want what is truly good for us. While no friend is perfect, a good friend brings us feelings of well-being and contentment. Christ's love abounds in a real friend.

On the other hand, a not-so-true friend often has his or her own interests in mind. Not-so-true friends often influence us to do things that make us feel uncomfortable or uneasy. Our behavior around these individuals makes us feel bad about ourselves. We tend not to like who we are when we are "under the influence" of not-so-true friends.

Going back to the analogy of the lifelong journey, real friends attempt to walk with us down the same road that Jesus walked. This road is often the more difficult path. It is usually less glamorous and appears less exciting. But people who live the values Jesus taught find their lives to be joy-filled and…anything but dull.

On the following page, honestly assess the quality of your closest friends. It is important to take a hard look at the people with whom we share our hearts and our time. During adolescence especially, friends tend to influence us more than family or Church—so it is essential that we open our eyes and see where they are leading us.

Think for a few moments—and then write honestly about your most important friends. Attempt to conclude with a statement or two about the quality and authenticity of these friendships. (Remember your spiritual journal is confidential—so be as honest as possible.)

Finally, let's take a brief look at the community of believers with whom you worship—your parish family. Along with your family and friends, your parish is an important source of support as you prepare for the sacrament of confirmation. The purpose of the "Parish Commitment Ceremony" is twofold. It makes the parish community aware of your preparation and asks the parish community to support you through prayer and encouragement.

Before responding to the following questions, read #781-782 of the *Catechism of the Catholic Church* which gives a marvelous description of the Church as the people of God. With these thoughts in mind, write about your own parish. Begin with its name and perhaps a brief history—then describe important aspects of your faith community. This may include physical aspects of the building and worship space, specific people who have helped the community grow, music you find meaningful, and so on. Also include any means by which you contribute to the community, whether directly through a special ministry or indirectly through prayer or service to a needy parishioner. If you are not yet involved in your parish, give some thought to small ways you can share your time or talent with your parish community.

_____
_____
_____
_____
_____
_____
_____
_____
_____
_____
_____
_____
_____

THE SACRAMENTS OF INITIATION

Our Introduction to the Life of the Church

Initiation is defined as "the rites, ceremonies, etc., observed in admitting a candidate into a society or organization." There are many forms of initiation—some formal, as when one joins the Boy or Girl Scouts—and some informal, as when one joins an athletic team. After committing oneself to a particular organization, one is expected to complete the proper forms and applications, attend meetings or practices, wear the organization's uniforms or adhere to the dress code, and generally participate in the activities of the group.

Consider an organization—athletic, social, service, or other—that you have been an active member of in the past. Whether it be formal or informal, describe that group's initiation process. Then discuss how this process eventually helped you to feel a "full" member of the organization.

_____
_____
_____
_____
_____
_____
_____
_____
_____

At this point, you have already been partially initiated into the life of the Catholic Church through your reception of the sacraments of baptism and first Eucharist. Begin this section of your journal by recording a few details about your experience of these sacraments. You may need to have your parents assist you.

Date of your baptism

Your age

Your godparents' names and their relationship to your family

Church (name and location)

Significant witnesses

Date of your first holy Communion

Your age

Church (name and location)

Significant witnesses

Significant details you remember

Scheduled date for your reception of the sacrament of confirmation

Your age

Church (name and location)

Person who will likely confirm you

Your sponsor or possible sponsors if you are undecided

What kind of moral framework would you have if you never knew Jesus? Would you have different friends? How would you celebrate special days like Christmas and Easter if Jesus was not part of your life? Would you view death differently?

In light of what you just wrote, do your best to respond to these questions:

What does your baptism mean to you?

_____
_____
_____
_____
_____
_____
_____
_____
_____
_____

What does it mean to have life in the Church?

_____
_____
_____
_____
_____
_____
_____
_____
_____
_____

It's time to examine a few of the basic "belief statements" of the Catholic Church—the Nicene Creed, the Apostles' Creed, the Ten Commandments, and the Eight Beatitudes.

Before turning your attention to these creeds and passages from Scripture, think a moment about the man, Jesus Christ, upon whose life, words, and teachings, we base our entire faith.

What image do you hold of the person Jesus? How would you describe the kind of man Jesus was during his earthly ministry?

___

If you could have witnessed one of Jesus' miracles or another important event in his life, which would it be? Why?

___

If Jesus lived on earth during the present time, what values do you believe he would have espoused? How would those values compare to the moral teachings of the Catholic Church?

___

Reread the Nicene Creed and the Apostles' Creed. Rewrite, in your own words, the statements you feel are most important. Remember to use language that is meaningful to you.

I believe in God…

Choose one of the Ten Commandments that you feel is especially important—and perhaps too often ignored by today's society. Rewrite the commandment in your own words, and explain why you believe it is especially relevant to our world today.

_____
_____
_____
_____
_____
_____
_____
_____

Choose one of the Eight Beatitudes from Matthew's Gospel that, again, is especially important or meaningful to you. Restate the beatitude in your own words, and explain why it holds special meaning for you.

_____
_____
_____
_____
_____
_____
_____
_____
_____
_____

The space on this page is for you to do some serious thinking and questioning. By now, you have a fairly firm understanding of the religious and moral teachings of the Catholic Church. After spending a few moments considering those teachings, write down any questions you have. Do any of the beliefs of the Church not make sense to you? Are there teachings set forth by the Church with which you do not agree? Why or why not?

Be honest with yourself and remember that it is okay—and even quite healthy—to ask questions. This is how we grow, learn, and mature. If you have serious doubts about your belief in the teachings of the Catholic Church, attempt to write down your concerns. Your "notes" could be very helpful should you seek the help of a priest or catechist.

My Doubts, My Questions, My Search for the Truth

A Brief History of the Sacrament

Taking a look at the history of a nation, a people, or a tradition helps us to better understand the present nature of that nation, people, or tradition. For example, it would be difficult to understand the country of Israel without examining the incredible history of the Jewish people. It would be next to impossible to understand the nature of race relations in the United States without studying the painful past of African Americans. Most Bible scholars tell us that learning about the cultural milieu of the biblical authors will greatly improve our understanding of sacred Scripture.

When reading the description of how confirmation was celebrated in the very early Church, there is a remarkable resemblance between second-century celebrations of the sacraments of initiation and modern Church Easter Vigil liturgies when new members are being "initiated" into the faith.

The fact that the Catholic Church has a rich history, which can be traced all the way back to Saint Peter, makes its traditions all the more meaningful. A study of Church history as a whole helps us to see that its most fundamental teachings have remained largely unchanged throughout the centuries. Still, in an attempt to better serve the people of God, the Church has seen changes in many areas, such as liturgy (in modern times, especially since Vatican II), the use and interpretation of sacred Scripture, and the role of the laity.

On the following pages, you will be asked to look at the history of your family (prior to your birth) and your personal history (in other words, the story of "you"). As with the Church, your history has played a big part in determining who you are today. The people and experiences of your past have greatly influenced the development of the unique and priceless you.

Write about the history of your family. Use the knowledge of your parents, and if possible, your grandparents to help you describe the lives of your immediate ancestors. Where were your grandparents and great-grandparents born? How did you come to live where you live today? What were the occupations of your grandparents and great-grandparents? Does your family (or did your family) operate a "family business" that has seen more than one generation? Did any of your ancestors experience traumatic life events such as slavery, a war, or the Great Depression? Write with as much detail as possible. Use additional paper or a notebook if additional space is desired.

_____
_____
_____
_____
_____
_____
_____
_____
_____
_____
_____
_____
_____
_____
_____
_____

Now write your personal history. Begin with your birth (when and where it occurred) and briefly tell about the important events of your life—moves from one city to another, the deaths or losses of loved ones, special attachments to pets, best friends through the years—any experience that has influenced or helped shape the person you are today. Again, use additional paper or a notebook if necessary.

All About Me

The sacrament of confirmation is an important Church tradition, one that has its roots in first- and second-century Christianity. What traditions are important in your family? How do you celebrate birthdays, Christmas, Easter, and other special events? Why are traditions important? How do they help bind families? How do Church traditions help bind the people of God?

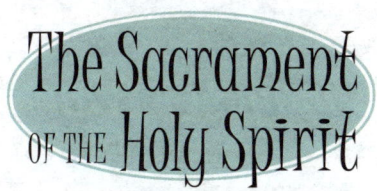

The Sacrament of the Holy Spirit

This activity concentrates on what the *Catechism of the Catholic Church* and sacred Scripture have to teach us about the nature of the Holy Spirit. With this background information in mind, it is time to focus on your own images of the Holy Spirit. Scripture uses the beautiful and mysterious word, **RUAH** to name the indescribable Spirit. Images of nature, also beautiful and mysterious, are often associated with the Spirit and the power of the Spirit. Examples include wind, fire, and water.

Think about these images. All have tremendous power. And yet, all are impossible for us to "grasp." We cannot hold them in our hands. But we feel the glorious touch of the wind. We *feel* the warmth of fire, and we can see its radiant light. We all know the delight of water quenching our thirst and bringing us, in a sense, back to life. These elements of nature—of God's own creation—help us gain a sense of how the Spirit moves us, works within us, and leads us to life.

On the following pages, you will be asked to journal about your experiences, your memories, and your feelings about wind, fire, and water. This would be a great place to create poetry or artwork. You might enjoy writing using a technique called "stream of consciousness" in which phrases, thoughts, ideas, and images just flow together to create an overall impression.

Be creative and free with your prose, poetry, and artwork! Be moved by the Spirit!

> "The Spirit of the Lord is upon me,
> because he has anointed me
> to bring good news to the poor.
> He has sent me to proclaim release to the captives and
> recovery of sight to the blind, to let the oppressed go free,
> to proclaim the year of the Lord's favor."
> Luke 4:18-19

Let the Spirit move you.

_____
_____
_____
_____
_____
_____
_____
_____
_____
_____
_____
_____

Let the Spirit move you.

_____
_____
_____
_____
_____
_____
_____
_____
_____
_____

Let the Spirit move you.

Holy Spirit, Bearer of Gifts

Church tradition teaches that the Spirit strengthens us for life's great journey through the bestowal of seven important gifts—wisdom, courage, reverence, understanding, right judgment, knowledge, and wonder and awe in God's Presence.

These are undoubtably unique gifts—gifts which cannot be purchased at any price. One does not have to be able to "afford" these gifts. They are offered to everyone who calls on the Spirit for the strength to follow in the footsteps of Jesus.

Reflect for a few moments on gifts you have received that have had a special and lasting value for you. Recall ways that others have touched your heart through thoughtful actions or gifts that are particularly creative or unique. Perhaps you were given an item that belonged to a beloved relative. Or a musical instrument that eventually became part of your very "being." Did you ever receive a gift that became a tool for creative expression, such as a camera or dancing shoes? Has anyone ever taken you on a trip that you will never forget or out for an evening that you will never forget? Have you ever been given a pet that became a "forever friend"?

Think for a moment. Is it true that most gifts of truly lasting value cannot be purchased at the mall? What makes these gifts have lasting value? How are these gifts similar to the gifts we receive from the Holy Spirit? Do they both somehow enrich our lives? Are they both, in some way, "food" for our great journey?

"You will receive power when the Holy Spirit has come upon you; and you will be my witnesses in Jerusalem, in all Judea and Samaria, and to the ends of the earth" (Acts of the Apostles 1:8).

A New Way to Look at Real Heroes

Scripture tells us that "all who are led by the Spirit of God are children of God" (Romans 8:14). The *Catechism* states that the gifts of the Spirit make us open to "obeying divine inspirations" (#1831). While reflecting on these ideas, call to mind people you truly admire and respect. Then focus on one particular individual who is a real hero to you. If possible, do not choose a "superstar." The emphasis here is not on accomplishment but rather on character. Consider the seven gifts of the Holy Spirit. It is quite possible that most real heroes possess and utilize one or more of the Spirit's gifts in extraordinary fashion.

Describe your hero, emphasizing the presence of the gifts (or fruits) of the Holy Spirit:

_____
_____
_____
_____
_____
_____
_____
_____
_____
_____
_____
_____
_____
_____
_____
_____

The following pages of your confirmation journal provide space for you to record your "assessment" of your life at the present time. Answer these questions very honestly. Remember your responses are confidential. The purpose is to help you evaluate your life and to then help you determine if you are satisfied with the direction you are going.

In the past several months, when did you feel happiest and most content with your life?

_____
_____
_____

In the past several months, when did you most experience feelings of discontentment and/or depression?

_____
_____
_____

Of your friends, who brings out "the best" in you? Who allows you to "be yourself" and who accepts you for the person you are?

_____
_____
_____

Of your friends, who makes you feel "inadequate"? Who encourages you to behave in ways that make you feel uncomfortable?

_____
_____
_____

If there was one area of your life you would like to change, what would it be? Specifically, what would you change? How would this change affect "the state" of your entire life?

_____
_____
_____

Take a close look at the gifts the Holy Spirit provides. Would any of these gifts be helpful in bringing about positive change in your life? If so, which gift and why?

_____
_____
_____

What do you see as your "strengths"? What do you like about yourself? Please do not feel that you are being boastful. God has given you unique and beautiful gifts, try not to ignore them.

_____
_____
_____
_____

Everyone experiences "ups and downs." Do you see your life as spiraling upward or downward? Do you feel you have control over the direction of your life? Do you believe that Jesus is with you always as he promised? If not, think of people you trust whom you can turn to for help and guidance...and seek them out. The gifts of the Spirit come to us most profoundly through God's people.

_____
_____
_____
_____

A Sacrament of Christian Witness

Consider a commitment to do the work of Jesus. While the previous lesson helped you discover more about yourself, it also gave you a framework from which to make decisions about the Christian witness you would enjoy. As you acknowledge your areas of strength (and weakness), you can see how your gifts can be used to build God's kingdom on earth.

In his Gospel, Saint Luke describes the baptism of Jesus and the coming of the Holy Spirit upon him (3:21-22). Jesus then sought out the quiet and solitude of the desert:

> **Jesus, full of the Holy Spirit, returned from the Jordan and was led by the Spirit in the wilderness... (Luke 4:1).**

King of Kings, 1961. MGM.
Jeffery Hunter as Jesus. Kobal Collection.

It is an interesting point that the Spirit led Jesus into the wilderness where he prayed, fasted, and was tempted by evil, before Jesus entered his public ministry. In this place of solitude, he prepared for this great commitment. After his retreat, Jesus returned to Galilee "filled with the power of the Spirit" (Luke 4:14).

Solitude and quiet are rarities in our modern world. We are a "plugged-in" society. Technology has given us televisions, stereos, computers, and even "hand-held" computer games. We are seldom without the phone—it will fit in our purses and our pockets. The miracle of modern technology keeps us in touch with everyone, it seems, except ourselves.

Time spent in solitude is absolutely essential to self-knowledge. It is also most conducive to prayer. How can we listen to God and sense the gentle "urgings" of the Holy Spirit if we constantly bombard ourselves with noise, activity, and people? We have largely become a people who fear being alone. We don't know what to "do" with solitude. When we finally get a moment alone, our first impulse is to flip on the television, computer, or radio.

How often do you choose instead to go for a long walk—alone and without headphones? How often do you opt to sit in your own backyard—quietly and alone? Do you ever take the time to silently lay in a hammock and stare at the heavens?

_____

_____

_____

    Use this page to describe your favorite "wilderness place"—a place you go when you wish to take refuge from the world. Where do you go to think when you have an important decision to make? Where do you go when you are feeling especially sad?

    Perhaps you have a quiet corner in your room...perhaps a favorite bench or hiking path in a nearby park. Wherever it might be, we all need a place where we can look into our hearts and listen to our inner voice. How often the Spirit will lead us to this place of solitude and peace—if we will only quiet ourselves enough to listen and follow.

    If you do not yet have a "wilderness place," write about a place you could establish as your own—and do your best to visit there several times a week. (If you choose a spot in your home, you might even make a little garden and keep it in your special room.)

_____

_____

_____

_____

_____

_____

_____

_____

_____

_____

It is generally true that we make time for what we love. If we love music, we probably make the time to listen to our favorite kind of music or to play an instrument. If we love to read, chances are, we spend time with our favorite books. If we love being with people, we likely have an active social life. And so on.

We can learn a lot about ourselves by examining how we choose to spend our time. This writing activity will help you focus on your personal interests and talents.

If you have a day to do anything you want to do, how will you spend your time? Imagine you have a reasonable amount of money and readily available transportation. From the day's beginning until its end, what will you do? Will you spend the day alone or with a particular friend or friends?

"If I Had a Day All to Myself…"

What kind of personality do you have? Are you a good organizer who likes to get involved with lots of different kinds of people? Or are you a person who prefers to work one-on-one or in very small groups?

_____
_____
_____
_____
_____
_____

What do you enjoy doing? (The paragraph you wrote on the previous page of this journal may help you to answer this question.)

_____
_____
_____
_____
_____
_____

What kind of demands do you already have on your time? (Consider commitments you have already made. How much time can you realistically give to your Christian service project?)

_____
_____
_____
_____
_____
_____

Signs and Symbols of the Sacrament of Confirmation

Ritual is important to the smooth functioning of our lives. We have daily rituals, nightly rituals, Sunday rituals, and holiday rituals. Whether we are aware of them of not, these set ways of doing things give meaning, predictability, and order to our existence. (Just imagine if your birthday arrived and no one planned any festivities or special meals....What if no one even bothered to bake a cake?)

Rituals are further enriched by signs and symbols. (Again, that birthday cake seems such a necessary part of birthday celebrations!) From the Easter egg to the wedding ring, symbols give our rituals something we can see, touch, and hold.

The Catholic Church's celebrations are rich in sign, symbol, and ritual. Symbols involve all our senses, remind us of the deeper mysteries of our faith, and add depth and meaning to our worship. Rituals help us know what to expect. They make us feel at home and give us a sense of great tradition. They, too, bring purpose and meaning to our worship.

Many of the symbols used in Catholic liturgical celebrations are images drawn from nature. Water is a central symbol, essential to the sacrament of baptism and to rites which give us the opportunity to renew our baptismal vows. Fire (light) is another powerful symbol taken from nature, used to "dispel the darkness" on Holy Saturday night.

Bring to mind other images from nature which serve as symbols in the Catholic tradition, such as a grain of wheat, the mustard seed, the pearl, the wood of the cross, the rainbow, and so on.

> "In human life, signs and symbols occupy an important place. As being(s) at once body and spirit, (we) express and perceive spiritual realities through physical signs and symbols.... Light and darkness, wind and fire, water and earth, the tree and its fruit speak of God and symbolize both [God's] greatness and [God's] nearness." (CCC, #1146-47)

Use drawings and/or prose and poetry to depict an image from nature which helps you to "express and perceive" a "spiritual reality." Select an image that is particularly beautiful and meaningful to you.

In this lesson, you are given the important task of making a banner to be used in the confirmation celebration. Select one of the following signs, symbols, or rituals: the Christian community assembled, the bishop, candidates for confirmation, the sponsors, the word of God, the prayer of the community, the laying on of hands, the anointing with chrism, or the Eucharist.

Use the lines below to write, in your own words, the meaning of the sign, symbol, or ritual you have selected.

The Meaning of...

Use this page to sketch a "rough draft" of your banner.

Simplicity is often the key to a powerful symbolic representation. Pencil in the colors you will use and your preferred art medium. Use words only if they will enhance your banner. Do not feel that you have to explain your symbol. Most importantly, enjoy yourself!

Celebration of the Sacrament of Confirmation

You should be familiar with the primary parts of the eucharistic celebration surrounding the sacrament of confirmation—from the gathering of the faith community to the final blessing. Remember that the confirmation rite involves the entire assembly. Those gathered in the church with you are not mere "spectators." Rather, they are witnesses to the sacrament and through their own faith, they support and empower you who are about to be confirmed. Just as special family celebrations—like birthdays—usually include friends and relatives outside of the immediate family, important Church celebrations—like first Eucharist, holy matrimony, and confirmation—welcome witnesses from outside of the immediate parish family. The sacrament of confirmation, in particular, emphasizes that we are part of the whole Church, the people of God.

The following pages of your spiritual journal ask you to take a closer look at some of the important words and prayers included in the Sacrament of Confirmation.

*All-powerful God, Father of our Lord Jesus Christ,
by water and the Holy Spirit
you freed your sons and daughters from sin and gave them new life.
Send your Holy Spirit upon them to be their helper and guide...*

(from the celebration of the Sacrament of Confirmation)

At the time of your baptism, you became "priest, prophet, and king." These are titles of great importance, but they include some awesome responsibilities.

What does it mean to be a "prophet" in today's world? How can you live as a prophet in today's world?

_____

_____

_____

_____

"N., be sealed with the Gift of the Holy Spirit."

(from the celebration of the Sacrament of Confirmation)

The Catechism of the Catholic Church explains that "the anointing with sacred chrism, perfumed oil consecrated by the bishop, signifies the gift of the Holy Spirit to the newly baptized, who has become a Christian, that is, one 'anointed' by the Holy Spirit....In the Roman liturgy the post-baptismal anointing announces a second anointing with sacred chrism to be conferred later by the bishop—confirmation, which will as it were 'confirm' and complete the baptismal anointing" (#1241-1242).

What does it mean to you to be "an anointed one"? In other words, how do you share in the role of Jesus Christ, the Anointed One?

_____

_____

_____

*The Holy Spirit came down upon the disciples
and set their hearts on fire with love:
may he bless you, keep you one in faith and love
and bring you to the joy of God's kingdom.*

(Final Blessing, from the celebration of the Sacrament of Confirmation)

You may not leave your confirmation celebration with your heart "on fire with love."

Still, how can your reception of this sacrament change the way you live your life?

_____
_____
_____
_____
_____
_____
_____
_____

Bill Wittman

Some Final Thoughts

Researching the Origin and Meaning of Your Confirmation and/or Baptismal Name

Your confirmation/baptismal name

Names you seriously considered:

_____
_____
_____

Why did you choose this name?

_____
_____
_____

Please write any information you have about your chosen name, especially regarding its origin and meaning:

_____
_____
_____
_____
_____
_____

Writing a Letter to Your Sponsor

Use this space to write a rough draft of a letter to your confirmation sponsor. Your teacher will give you further directions for writing this letter, but be sure to include the reasons you chose this particular person to be your spiritual guide. (And remember to express your gratitude!)

Date

Dear,

(closing and name)

This page is provided for you to write a rough draft of your letter to the bishop. Use the sample letter from your student handout as a guide, but do not copy it. Your letter should include the following points:

1. Express your desire to be confirmed.
2. State why you would like to be confirmed.
3. State how you have prepared for the sacrament.
4. List ways you intend to serve your brothers and sisters in Christ.
5. Express your gratitude and appreciation.

And just as importantly, write from your heart!

Date

Dear Bishop N.,

_____
_____
_____
_____
_____
_____
_____
_____

(closing and name)

Confirmation candidate of (parish)

Confirmation Candidate
RETREAT DAY

Session One
Reflection Questions

Reflect on the natural world and study the details and subtleties of nature. Think about what you can learn from nature.

1. Did you see signs of rebirth and reawakening in the natural world? How can you relate the change from winter to spring to your life?
2. Can the sacrament of confirmation be a chance for rebirth in your life? How?
3. Reflect on who you are right now. What are your strengths? What are your shortcomings? What do you like to do in your spare time? What do you do that gives you a sense of self-fulfillment? When do you feel happiest? When do you feel down or confused? Who are your favorite people? Who are your heroes?

Session Two
Reflection Questions

We must serve one another if we are to be followers of Christ. Jesus makes it so clear: "You also should do."

1. Describe the various ministries within the Church that are now or will soon become service options for you. For example: cantor, choir member, lector, hospitality minister.

2. Describe possible service options available through your school. For example: tutor, library assistant, assistant coach.

3. Describe ways you can serve others in your neighborhood or community.

4. In the first session, you described yourself—your interests, talents, shortcomings, and so on. With your own interests and talents in mind, come up with one or two ways that you might effectively serve others. Think simply and realistically.